to horse around
to play in a rowdy way

monkey business
silly behavior

THERE'S A FROG IN MY THROAT!
440 Animal Sayings a Little Bird Told Me

written by
Loreen Leedy & Pat Street

illustrated by
Loreen Leedy

lucky duck
fortunate person

Holiday House
New York

meow!

It's the cat's meow!
It's terrific!

to turn turtle
to turn upside down

We love animal sayings! Sayings pack a lot of meaning into a few words. Plus, it's just more fun to say "It's raining cats and dogs" than "It's raining hard."

Every language has its own unique sayings. For this book, we collected 440 of our favorite animal sayings in English. As you will see, many of them compare people to animals.

A **simile** makes a comparison using the word *like* or the word *as*. If someone is "as quiet as a mouse," that person is silent. (Mice aren't noisy.)

A **metaphor** also makes a comparison, but without *like* or *as*. If someone is a "night owl," he or she likes to stay up late. (Owls are active at night.)

An **idiom** doesn't mean exactly what the words say. For example, "She has butterflies in her stomach" doesn't mean she's eaten some butterflies! Instead, it means "She feels nervous."

A **proverb** gives advice about how to act in daily life. For example, to advise someone not to exaggerate a problem, you can say, "Don't make a mountain out of a molehill."

We fit as many animal sayings into these pages as we could—even a few about feathers and shells and fur and tails. Most of these sayings are well known, but we think some will be new to you. We included one common meaning for each saying. (Some have more than one meaning.)

Happy reading! We hope you will enjoy this book "till the cows come home"—for a very long time!

See you later, alligator!
Loreen Leedy and Pat Street

It's not a fit night out for man or beast.
The weather is terrible.

I killed two birds with one stone.
I got two things done with one action.

woolgathering
daydreaming

2

contents

Let's tie on the old feed bag.
Let's eat.

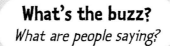

What's the buzz?
What are people saying?

It's the bee's knees!
It's terrific!

I put my head in the lion's mouth.
I took a big risk.

3

This place is going to the dogs.
Things are getting worse and worse.

dog-eared page
folded page corner

Let sleeping dogs lie.
Leave old problems alone.

Stop hounding me!
Stop pestering me!

Hot dog!
Wow!

You're barking up the wrong tree.
You've got the wrong idea.

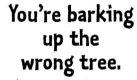

You can't teach an old dog new tricks.
It's harder for an older person to learn new things.

His bark is worse than his bite.
He's not as fierce as he seems.

It's a dog-eat-dog world.
Life can be brutally competitive.

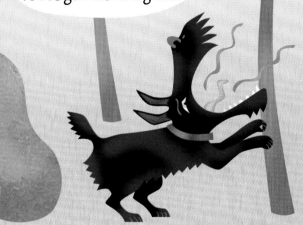

You lie like a dog.
You're telling a lie.

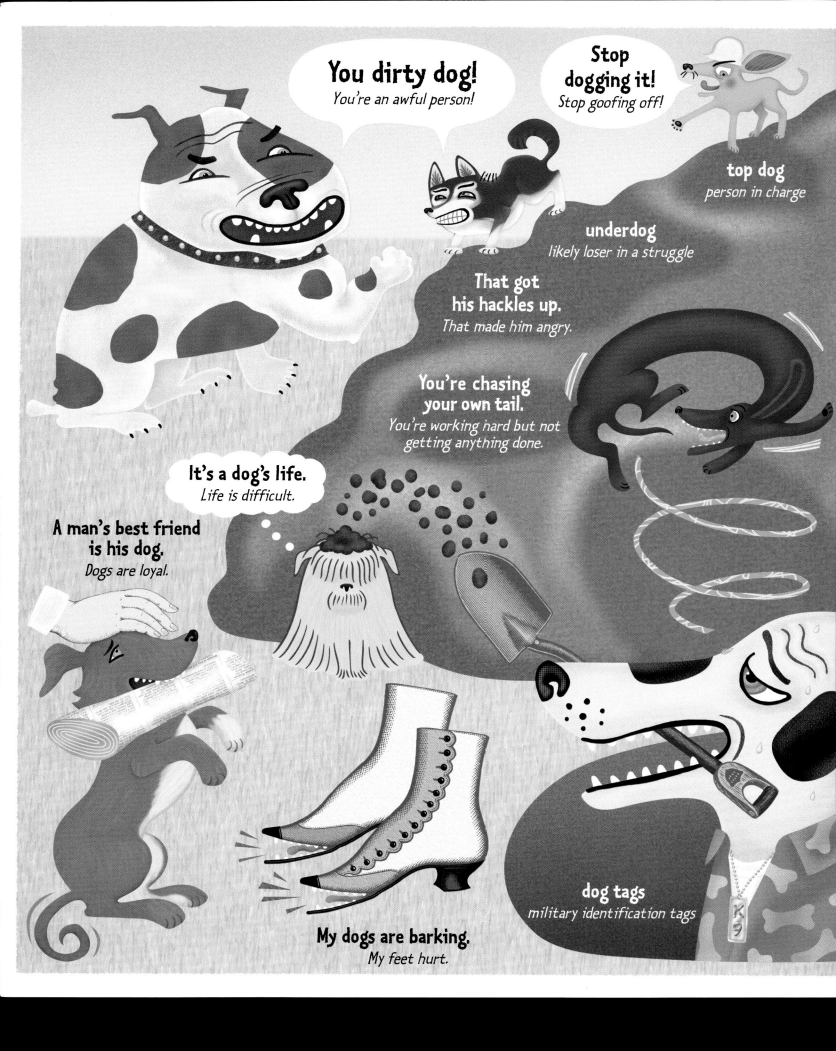

The tail is wagging the dog. *A small part is controlling the whole thing.*

They fight like cats and dogs. *They have fierce arguments.*

The fur is going to fly. *There will be a big fight.*

They put on a dog-and-pony show. *They gave us a fancy sales pitch.*

to do the doggie paddle *to swim like a dog*

It's a three-dog night. *It's very cold.*

It's raining cats and dogs.
It's raining hard.

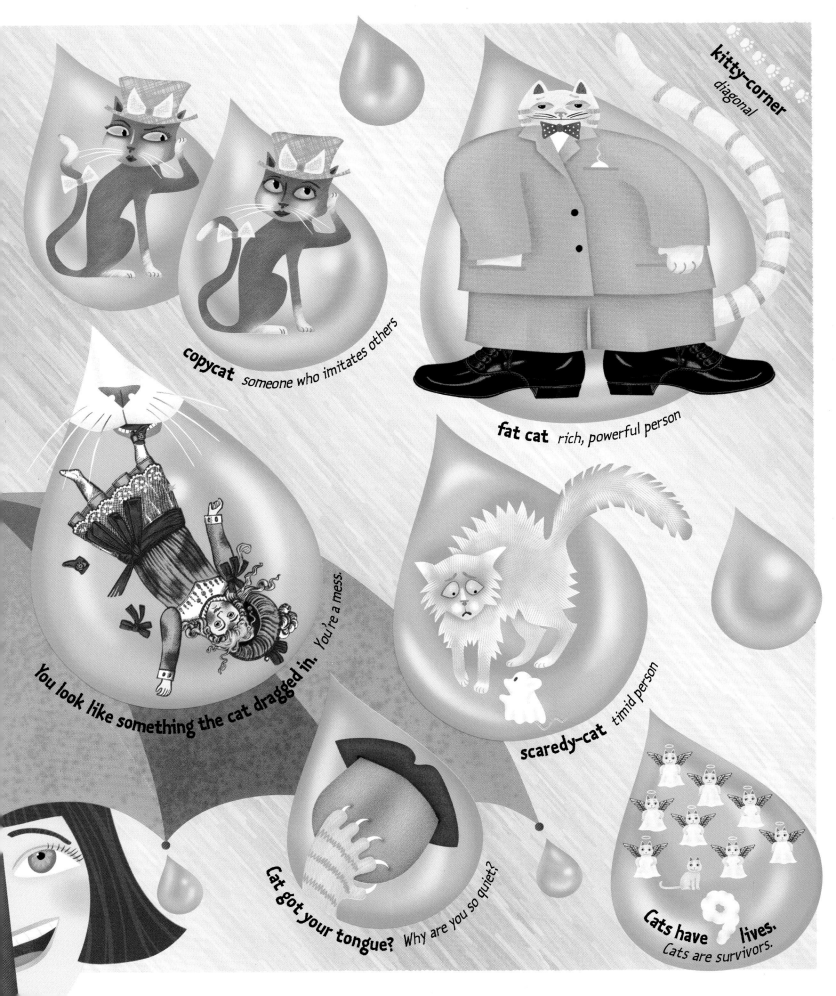

copycat *someone who imitates others*

fat cat *rich, powerful person*

You look like something the cat dragged in. *You're a mess.*

scaredy-cat *timid person*

Cat got your tongue? *Why are you so quiet?*

Cats have 9 lives. *Cats are survivors.*

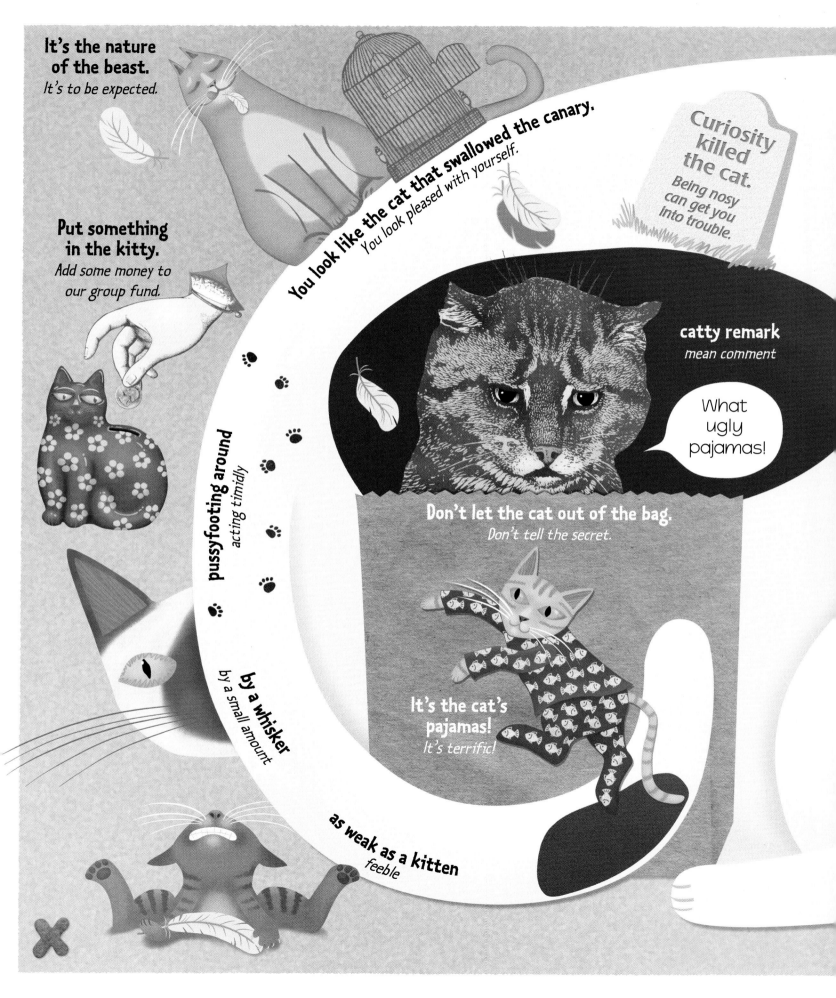

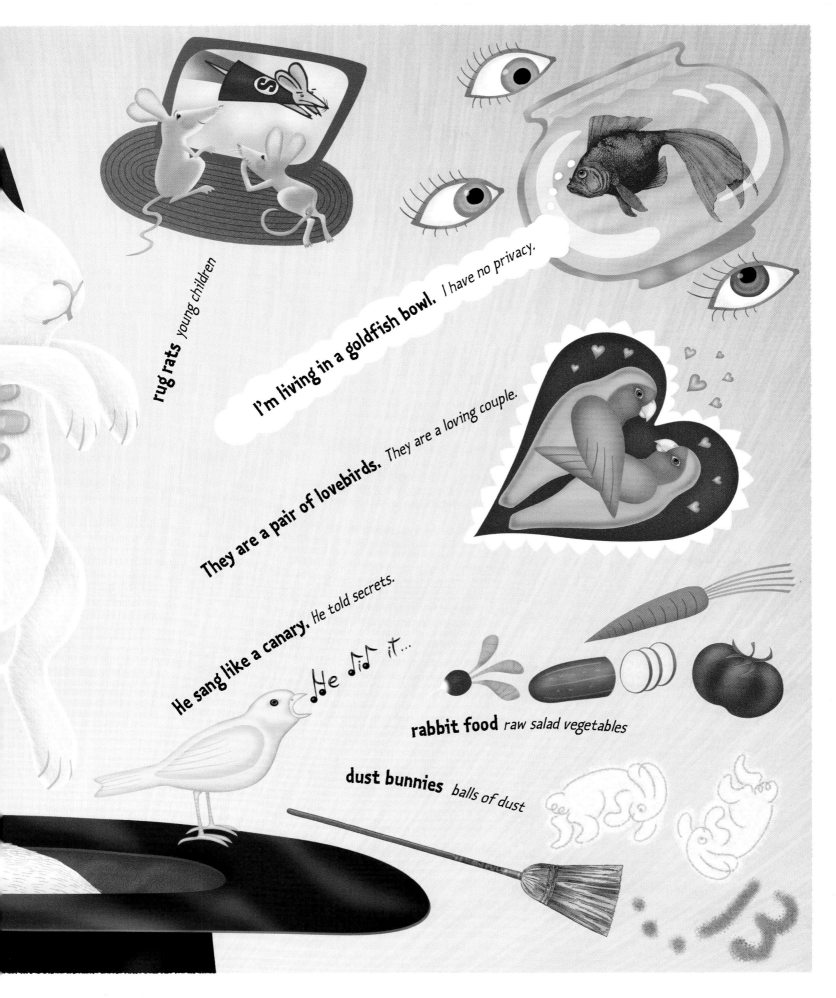

rug rats *young children*

I'm living in a goldfish bowl. *I have no privacy.*

They are a pair of lovebirds. *They are a loving couple.*

He sang like a canary. *He told secrets.*

rabbit food *raw salad vegetables*

dust bunnies *balls of dust*

I don't want to hear another peep out of you!
Be quiet!

There's nobody here but us chickens.
We're the only ones here.

You're letting the fox guard the henhouse.
You're putting the wrong person in charge.

Peep!

as mad as a wet hen
furious

She gets up with the chickens.
She wakes up early in the morning.

She is first in the pecking order.
She has the top rank in our group.

chicken feed
small amount of money

17

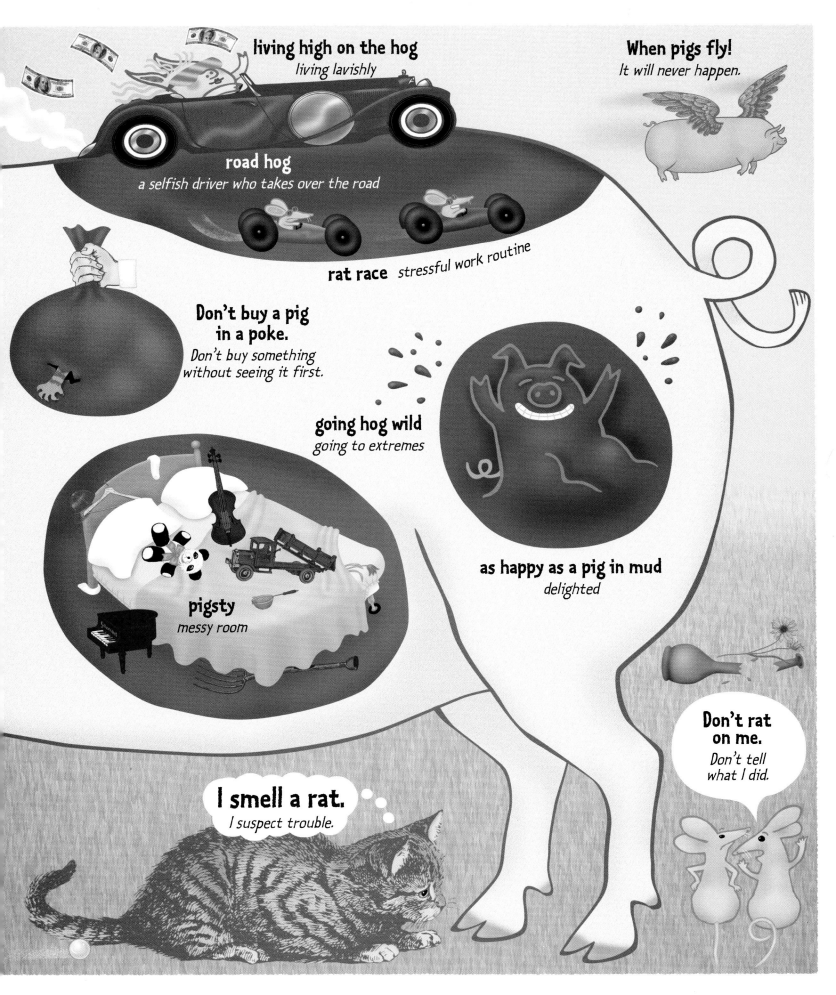

It's like waving a red flag in front of a bull.
It's something that will make him very angry.

He's like a bull in a china shop.
He's very clumsy.

Were you raised in a barn?
You are so rude!

cash cow
profitable business

I'm on the horns of a dilemma.
I have to make a tough choice.

as dark as the inside of a cow
pitch-black

cowlick
tuft of hair that sticks out

bullheaded
obstinate

Big hat, no cattle.
He is pretending to be a big shot.

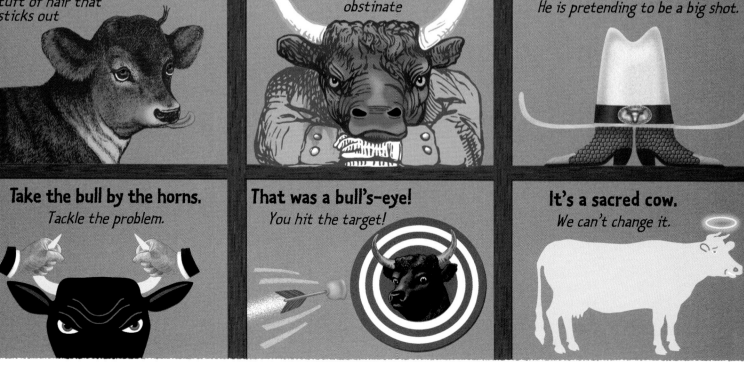

Take the bull by the horns.
Tackle the problem.

That was a bull's-eye!
You hit the target!

It's a sacred cow.
We can't change it.

He's a wolf in sheep's clothing.
He's an enemy pretending to be a friend.

as innocent as a lamb
blameless

scapegoat
innocent person who gets blamed

She pulled the wool over his eyes.
She fooled him.

Separate the sheep from the goats.
Divide the good from the bad.

to butt heads
to argue fiercely

That will get his goat.
That will make him angry.

in two shakes of a lamb's tail
quickly

sheepish
embarrassed

to butt in
to intrude

Butt out!
Mind your own business!

to get fleeced
to be swindled

23

That's just ducky!
That's just great!

Get your ducks in a row.
Get organized.

Quack!

If it looks like a duck, walks like a duck, and quacks like a duck, it's a DUCK!
It's obvious!

DUCKS 3
GEESE

goose egg
zero

There's a frog in my throat!
My throat is hoarse!

Ribbet!

What's sauce for the goose is sauce for the gander.
If you can do it, so can I.

We're dead ducks.
We're going to lose.

My goose is cooked.
I'm in trouble.

odd duck
peculiar person

24k

Don't kill the goose that lays the golden eggs.
Don't destroy the source of your good fortune.

She fawns on him.
She slavishly tries to please him.

to lock horns
to disagree

He is crazy like a fox.
He seems foolish, yet he is outsmarting everyone.

as sly as a fox
clever

What are your demands?

Unfair!

wolfing down food
eating too fast

cub reporter
journalist who is new on the job

dumb bunny
stupid person

Put a tail on him.
Send a spy to follow him secretly.

wildcat strike
unauthorized work stoppage

eager beaver
enthusiastic person

busy beaver
hard worker

to keep the wolf from the door
to provide food for one's family

He's a lone wolf.
He likes to be alone.

Grrrrr!

She threw me to the wolves.
She abandoned me in a bad situation.

29

I've seen the elephant.
I've seen more than enough.

When you hear hoofbeats, think horses, not zebras.
Try the simple solution first.

They have the herd instinct.
They follow the crowd.

There's an elephant in the room.
There's a big problem nobody wants to face.

white elephant
fancy thing no one wants

Don't bury your head in the sand like an ostrich.
Don't hide from reality.

She has a memory like an elephant.
She won't forget.

The leopard can't change his spots.
A person's nature will stay the same.

zebra crossing
striped crosswalk

It's an 800-pound gorilla.
It's an uncontrollable problem.

It's more fun than a barrel of monkeys.
It's very enjoyable.

as brave as a lion
courageous

Ha! Ha! Ha!

to lionize someone
to treat someone like a celebrity

to laugh like a hyena
laughing loudly

the lion's share
the biggest portion

30

Don't let the camel get its nose under the tent.
Don't let something bad get started.

I have a tiger by the tail.
This problem is huge.

He is a paper tiger.
He seems strong, but he is actually weak.

grease monkey
mechanic

monkeyshines
mischievous tricks

to go ape
to act wildly

It threw a monkey wrench into our plans.
It ruined our plans.

They made a monkey out of me.
They made me look foolish.

monkey suit
tuxedo

monkey see, monkey do
to copy what other people do

kangaroo court
a court that ignores the law

It's a dinosaur.
It's out of date.

It's neither fish nor fowl.
It doesn't fit easily into any category.

fossil
old person or thing

31

bird's-eye view
view from overhead

Keep an eagle eye on it.
Watch it carefully.

round-robin
project that's completed as different people add to it step-by-step

I'm as free as a bird.
There's nothing I have to do right now.

It's as light as a feather. *It weighs very little.*

You could've knocked me down with a feather.
I was very surprised.

Birds of a feather flock together.
Similar people stick together.

I was sent on a wild-goose chase.
I was asked to search for something that couldn't be found.

Don't ruffle any feathers.
Don't upset anyone.

stool pigeon
police informer

Just for a lark just for fun

as happy as a lark cheerful

to wing it
to improvise

crow's-feet
wrinkles in the corners of the eyes

I had to eat crow.
I had to admit I was wrong.

crow's nest
lookout platform

as the crow flies in a straight line

She is a social butterfly.
She goes to lots of parties.

I have butterflies in my stomach.
I feel nervous.

as mad as a hornet
furious

You'll catch more flies with honey than with vinegar.
You'll get what you want by being nice, not by being mean.

What's the Buzz? HONEY

BLUE LABEL VINEGAR
CURTICE BROTHERS CO.
ROCHESTER, N.Y. U.S.A.

to stir up a hornet's nest
to start a great deal of trouble

I was drawn like a moth to a flame.
I was fascinated.

moth-eaten
shabby

cocooning
retreating to the privacy of home

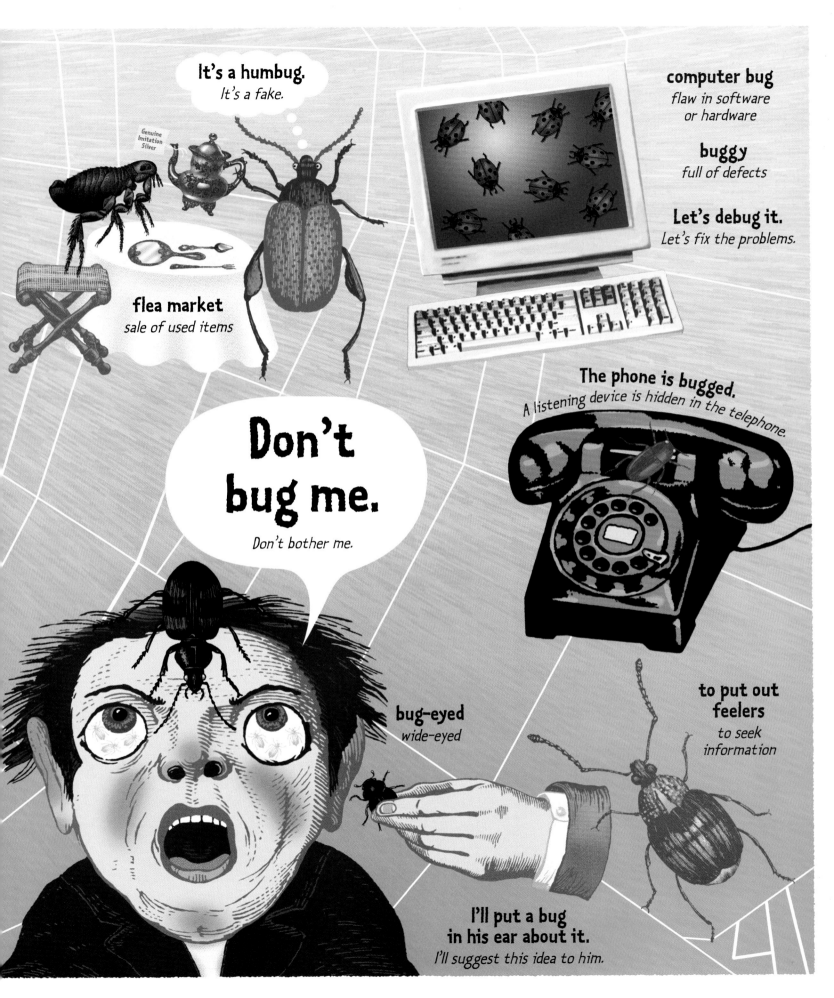

I feel like a fish out of water.
I feel out of place.

See you later, alligator!
Good-bye for now!

to cry crocodile tears
to pretend to be sorry

under the WAVES

Something smells fishy.
I suspect wrongdoing.

This is a fine kettle of fish.
This is a predicament.

You're smart.

You're pretty.

Poor me.

You're nice.

You're sweet.

She is fishing for compliments.
She is trying to get praise.

to flounder around
to fumble and struggle

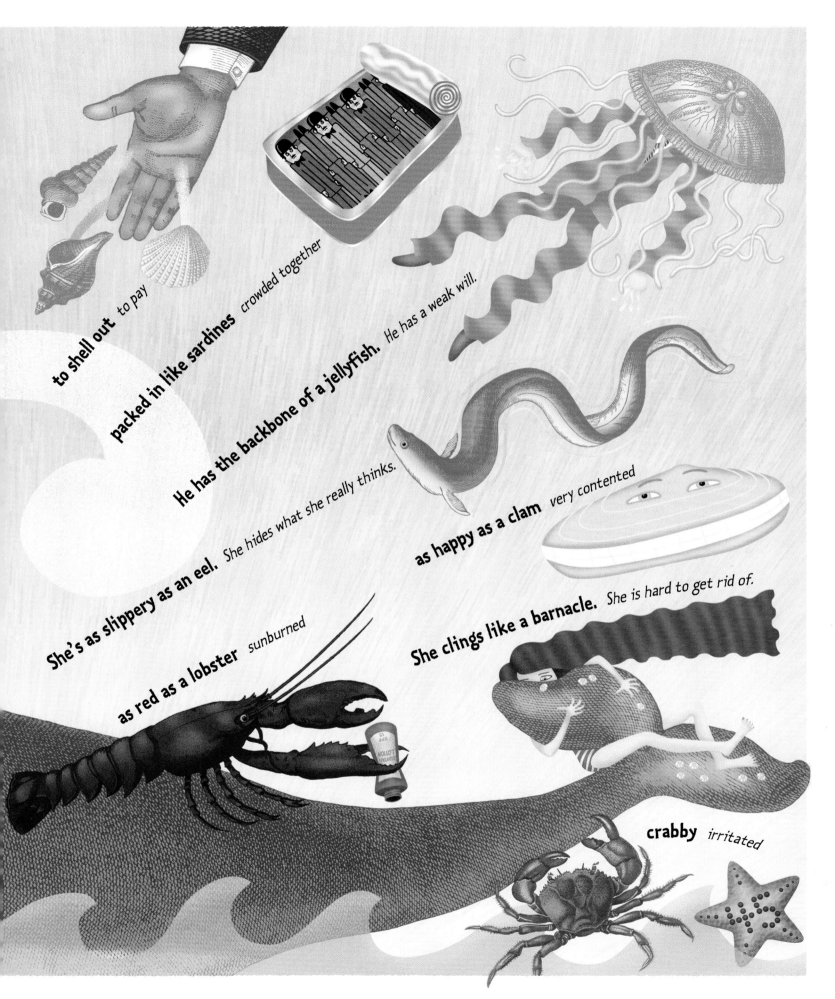

to shell out to pay

packed in like sardines crowded together

He has the backbone of a jellyfish. He has a weak will.

She's as slippery as an eel. She hides what she really thinks.

as happy as a clam very contented

as red as a lobster sunburned

She clings like a barnacle. She is hard to get rid of.

crabby irritated

**If wishes were horses,
then beggars would ride.**
Desire alone won't make dreams happen.

pet project
favorite project

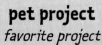

My crayon broke again!

pet peeve
repeated complaint

teacher's pet
favored student

46

**the black sheep
of the family**
the worst member of the family

WANTED

catcalls
loud yells of disapproval

Boo!
Boo!
Boo!

She wouldn't hurt a fly.
She is gentle.

The best-laid plans of mice and men oft go astray.
Even careful plans can go wrong.

I'll be a monkey's uncle!
I'm amazed!

It's driving me batty.
I'm frustrated with it.

I'm as blind as a bat.
My vision is poor.

donkey work
hard physical labor

For my feline friends—
Esme, Deli, Abby, Cleo, and Photon
L. L.
And for mine—
Skeezix and Dunkelman
P. S.

Text copyright © 2003 by Loreen Leedy and Pat Street
Illustrations copyright © 2003 by Loreen Leedy
All Rights Reserved
Printed in the United States of America
www.holidayhouse.com

Library of Congress Cataloging-in-Publication Data

Leedy, Loreen.
There's a frog in my throat: 440 animal sayings a little bird told me
by Loreen Leedy and Pat Street; illustrated by Loreen Leedy.—1st ed.
p. cm.
Includes index.
ISBN: 0-8234-1774-3 (hardcover)
ISBN: 0-8234-1819-7 (paperback)
1. English language—Terms and phrases—Juvenile literature.
2. Zoology—Nomenclature (Popular)—Juvenile literature.
3. Animals—Folklore—Juvenile literature.
4. Figures of speech—Juvenile literature. [1. English language—Terms and phrases.
2. Figures of speech. 3. Animals—Folklore.]
I. Street, Pat. II. Title.

PE1583.L39 2003
428.1—dc21   2002068920

I'm bullish.
I think stock market prices will go up.

I'm bearish.
I think stock market prices will go down.

the tail end
the very end

48